# ERIC CARLE'S
## BOOK OF MANY
## THINGS

PUFFIN BOOKS

UK | USA | Australia | Canada | India | Ireland | New Zealand | South Africa

Puffin Books is part of the Penguin Random House group of companies whose addresses can be
found at global.penguinrandomhouse.com.

www.penguin.co.uk          www.puffin.co.uk          www.ladybird.co.uk

Penguin
Random House
UK

First published 2018
001
Copyright © Eric Carle LLC, 2018

The moral right of Eric Carle has been asserted

Printed and bound in China

A CIP catalogue record for this book is available from the British Library

ISBN: 978–0–141–37436–9

Eric Carle's name and his signature logotype are trademarks of Eric Carle
To find out more about Eric Carle and his books, please visit **eric-carle.com**
To learn about The Eric Carle Museum of Picture Book Art, please visit **carlemuseum.org**

All correspondence to:
Puffin Books,
Penguin Random House Children's,
80 Strand, London WC2R 0RL

MIX
Paper from
responsible sources
FSC® C018179

Penguin Random House is committed to a
sustainable future for our business, our readers
and our planet. This book is made from Forest
Stewardship Council® certified paper.

# ERIC CARLE'S BOOK OF MANY THINGS

PUFFIN

# THINGS IN THIS BOOK

## THINGS YOU SEE

In the garden · In the sea
On the farm · At home · Weather · In the wild
Things that go · Creepy-crawlies

 ## THINGS YOU EAT

Fruit · Everyday food · Party food

## THINGS YOU LEARN

Opposites · Numbers
Shapes · Patterns

 ## COLOURFUL THINGS

Red · Blue · Yellow · Green
Pink · Orange · Black and white · Multi-coloured!

## THINGS ABOUT YOU

Your body · Moves you can make · What you wear
Things you can do · Feelings · Having fun with friends!

# THINGS YOU SEE

# IN THE GARDEN

grass

tree

bee

ball

flowers

ladybird

**lobster**

**walrus**

**narwhal**

**seahorse**

**jellyfish**

**seaweed**

**reeds**

# IN THE SEA

octopus

# ON THE FARM

crows

farmer

chick

cow

turkey

duck

horse

egg

sheep

lamb

plate

dog

chair

picture

clock

table

cat

# AT HOME

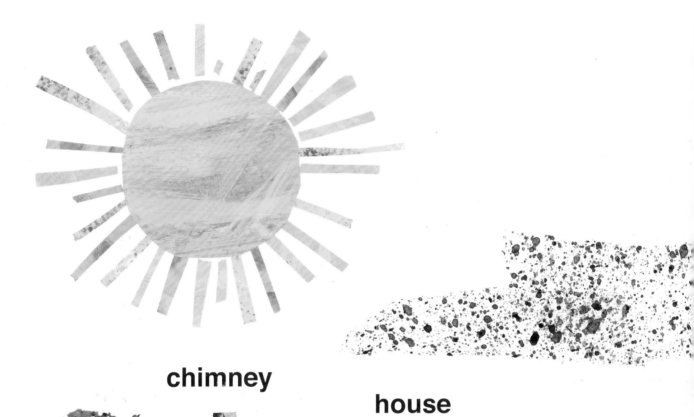

chimney

house

# WEATHER

wind

sun

cloud

snowflake

rain

rainbow

lightning

# IN THE WILD

snake

rhinoceros

lion

zebra

bear

hippopotamus

monkey

elephant

**aeroplane**

**truck**

**car**

**train**

**lorry**

# THINGS THAT GO

boat

# CREEPY-CRAWLIES

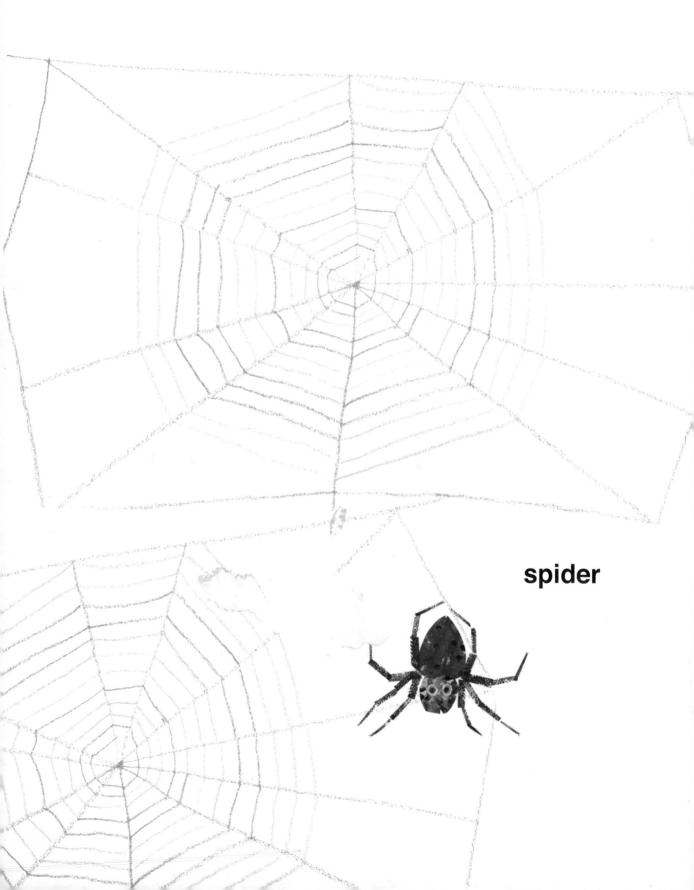

spider

firefly

cricket

snail

caterpillar

fly

beetle

ant

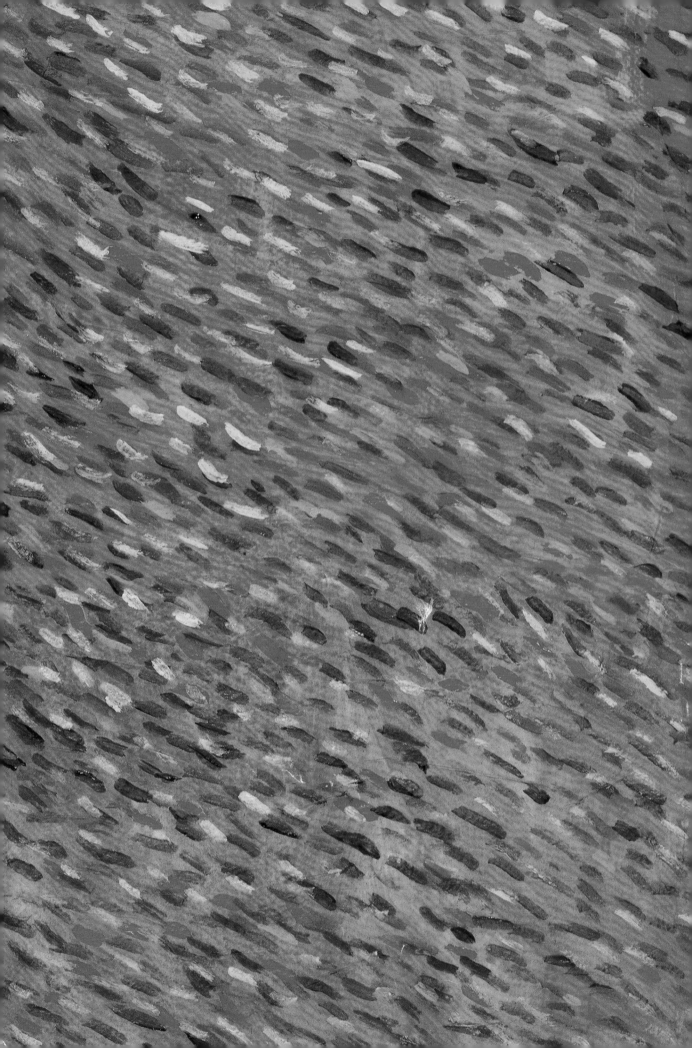

# THINGS YOU EAT

# FRUIT

watermelon

banana

grapes

lime

lemon

pineapple

kiwi

strawberry

fish

honey

bread

chicken

roast beef

spaghetti

green beans

# EVERYDAY FOOD

milk

# PARTY FOOD

cake

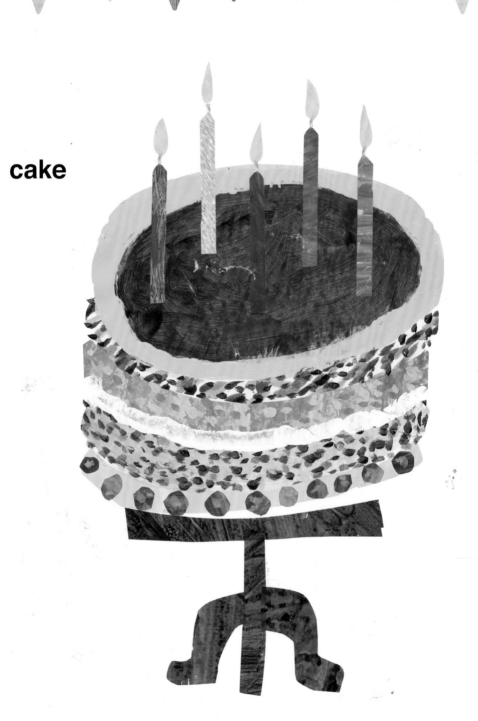

muffin

cheese

pie

ice cream

sausage

chocolate

# THINGS YOU LEARN

# OPPOSITES

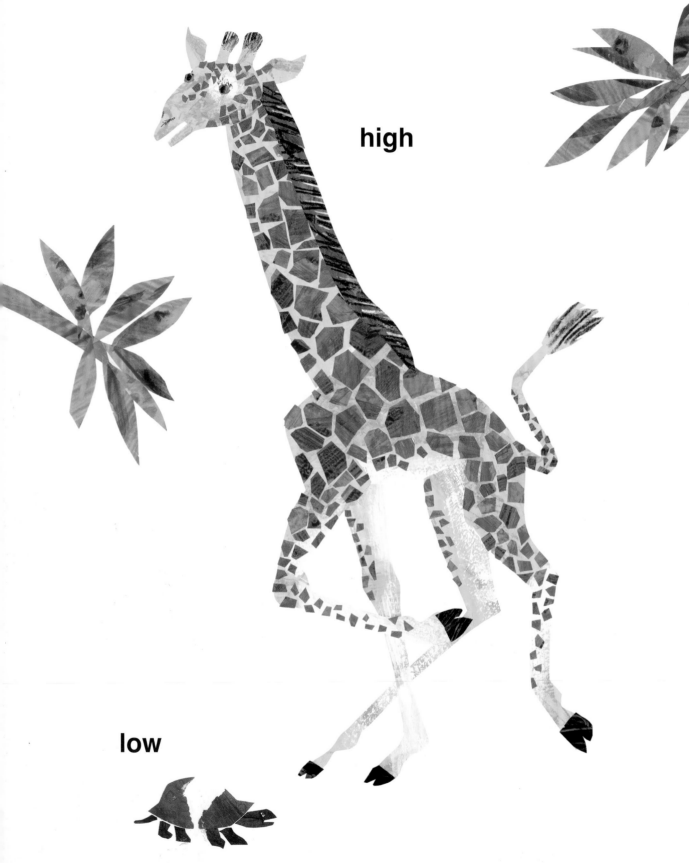

high

low

day

night

lots

few

soft

spiky

big

small

sweet

sour

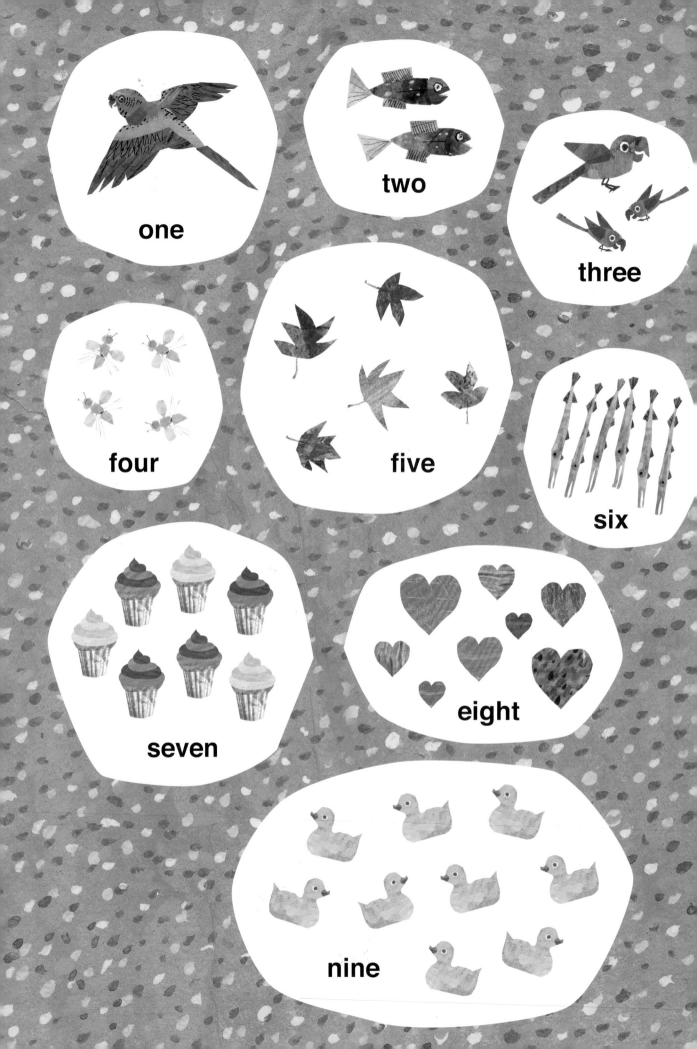

one

two

three

four

five

six

seven

eight

nine

# NUMBERS

ten

# SHAPES

circles

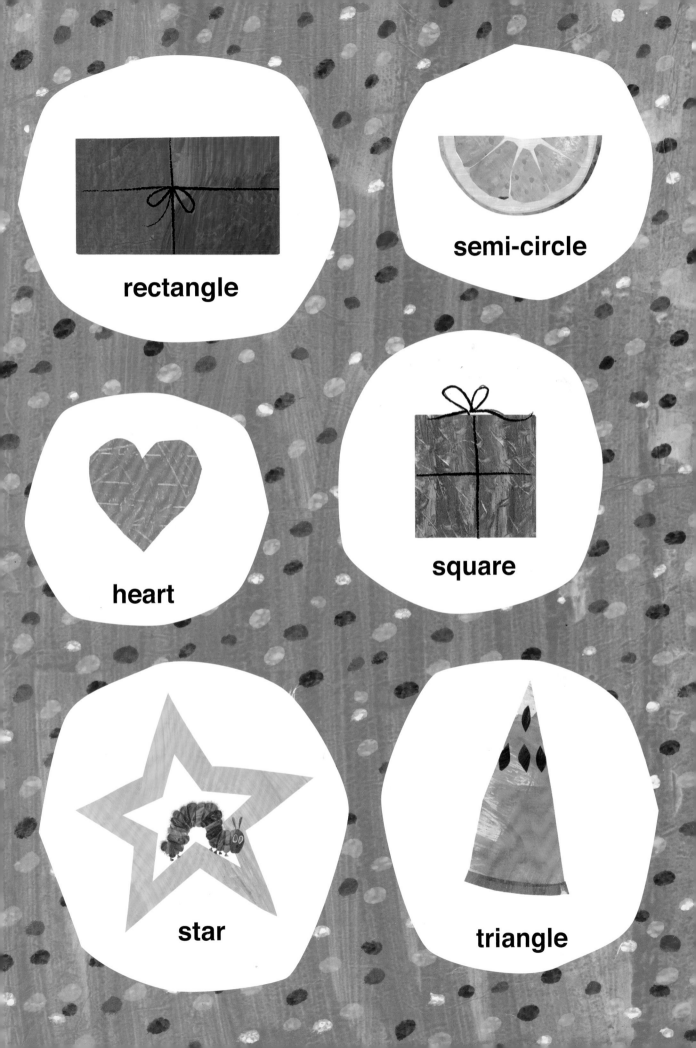

**rectangle**

**semi-circle**

**heart**

**square**

**star**

**triangle**

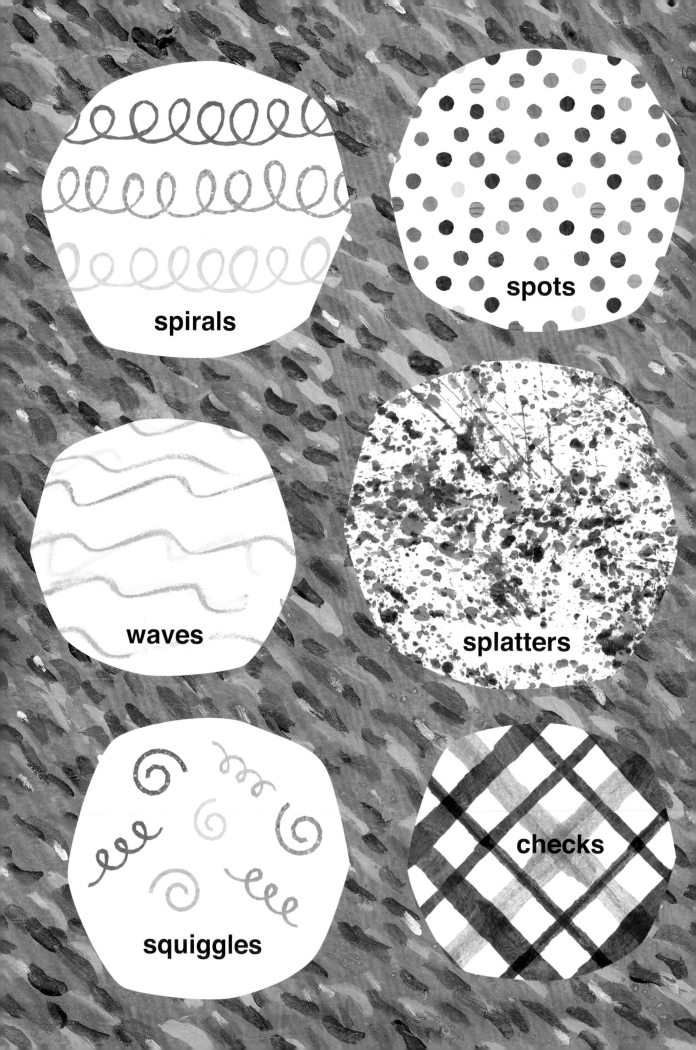

spirals

spots

waves

splatters

squiggles

checks

# PATTERNS

stripes

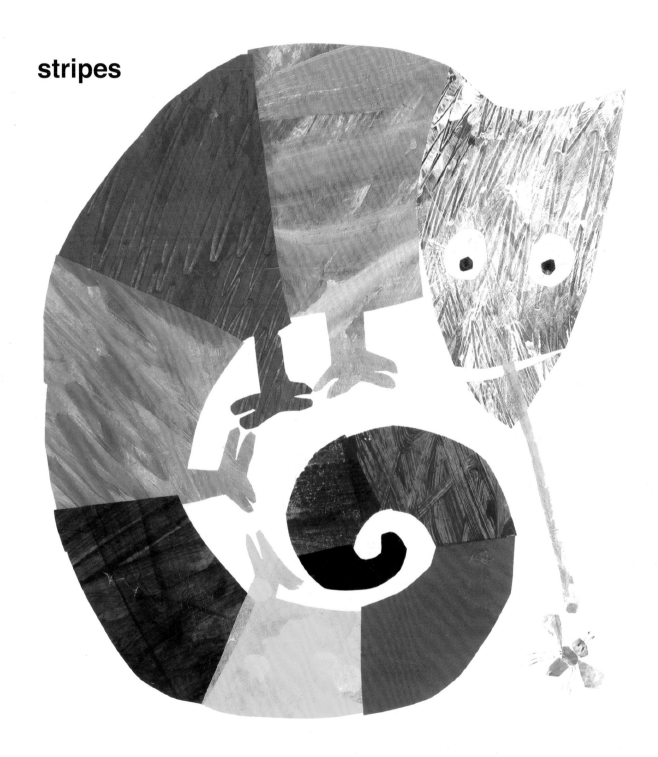

# COLOURFUL THINGS

# RED

fox

cherries

bag

squirrel

kangaroo

apple

**peacock**

**bird**

**plum**

**dragonfly**

**sea**

# BLUE

dolphin

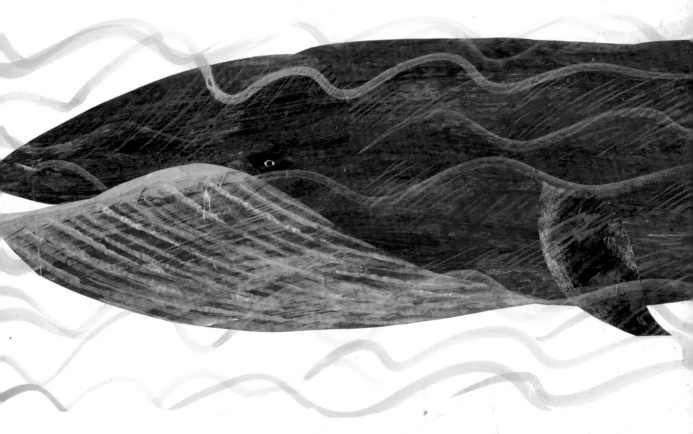

whale

YELLOW

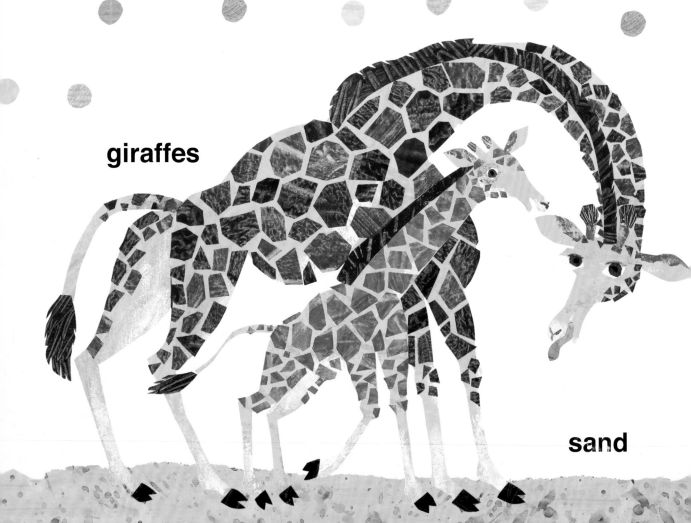

giraffes

sand

leopard

rubber duck

sunflower

honeybee

lions

leaf

turtle

holly

pear

lizard

gherkin

frog

# GREEN

crocodile

# PINK

blossom

cupcake

pig

flamingo

# ORANGE

**goldfish**

**carrots**

**orange**

skunk

panther

panda

goat

swan

penguin

# BLACK AND WHITE

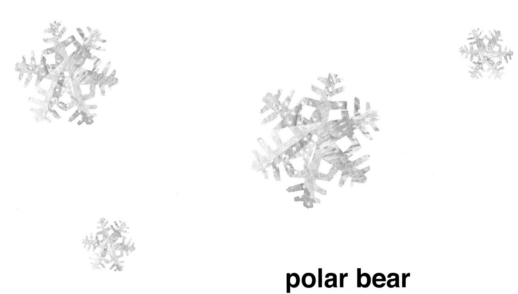

polar bear

# MULTI-COLOURED!

parrot

presents

THINGS ABOUT YOU

# YOUR BODY

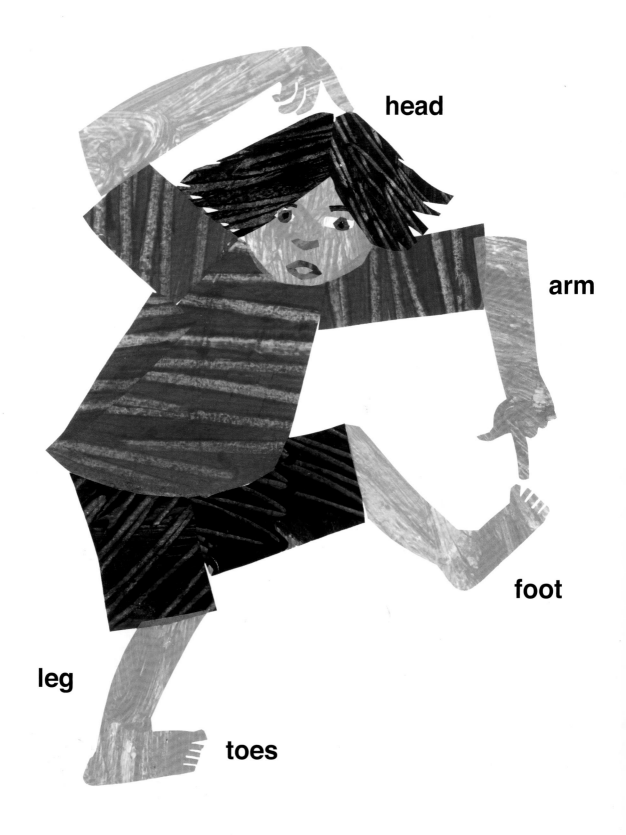

head

arm

foot

leg

toes

shoulder

knee

tummy

hand

dance

run

wiggle

kick

clap

handstand

# MOVES YOU CAN MAKE

**bend**

# WHAT YOU WEAR

dungarees

trousers

dress

T-shirt

shoes

hat

glasses

vest

boots

paint

look

sleep

draw

read

touch

# THINGS YOU CAN DO

sledge

**hungry**

**full up**

**tired**

**angry**

**sad**

**happy**

# FEELINGS

loved

# HAVING FUN WITH FRIENDS!

share

**hug**

**celebrate**

**smile**

**dress up**

**talk**

**play**

# Now, can you name
# all these things?